It's Pretty Simple...

but...

It's Never Easy

Helping Families For Over 30 Years – This Realtor Shares It All

It's Pretty Simple...
but...
It's Never Easy

Helping Families For Over
30 Years – This Realtor
Shares It All

Donna Rausch

Printed in the United States of America

First Printing, 2015

ISBN: 978-1500716639

This is dedicated to the people who come into my office thinking that selling real estate will be easy, and a quick way to make a million bucks - and to Steve, Karyn and Jon WHO KNOW THE REAL TRUTH.

Thank you.

YOU WANT TO SELL WHAT?
Real Estate.

Why ????

Following is a collection of how to's, why not's, and, there must be an easier way....

Index of Insights

YOU WANT TO SELL WHAT???

Real Estate.

Why?

I love houses.

Great! You love houses. Wonderful! That will go down in the archives of common sense right next to "Why yes, Virginia, there is a Santa Claus" and "Frankly Scarlet, I don't give a damn."

The love of the product. The thrill of the chase. The pride of success. Truly I cannot imagine a profession (or hobby) that satisfies as many of your natural instincts. You get to help. You get to serve. You get to complain. You get to whine while paying quarterly income taxes, and of course you get to "lunch".

Hold on, I'm getting ahead of things here. No need to bore you with the details until I am able to reel you in the same way I was reeled in — hook, line, and sinker. I took the bait and have never looked back....until now.

The opportunity to help people find a dream is one of the most rewarding sides of this profession. Nothing compares to the feeling when a first time homeowner thanks you for being there every step of the journey and for helping to make it all possible.

YOU'RE PERFECT FOR THIS

That's what I was told by my former Realtor and my friend; the person who diligently sold my home and proceeded to sell me another. She showed me every home I wanted to see. She took me to see homes on "caravan" where we had lunch. She showed me homes I had no interest in. She showed me homes I could not afford and she showed me JUNK!!

We had a good time. Our kids got along really well. (That should have been one big indication.....if you have a job where you can include your kids and you're not a daycare provider.....what are you doing? Was this a real job? Could I do this? You betcha!! It had my name written all over it in capital letters.)

The discussions my husband and I had with regard to this new career path lasted quite a while.

What's the initial cost?

- Next to nothing.

Who'll watch the kids?

- No problem. I'll bring them along.

What about me?

- Sweetie, you'll never know I'm doing this. I'll be home every night and the weekends will still be our "family time".

Where do you expect to find people who want to buy a house?

- We've both lived in this town since we were born - we know everybody. This is a no-brainer. I'll have customers coming out of my ears!

Finally... *OK. As long as it won't cost much, you'll still have the kids as your priority and I will never know you're gone – try it. I think you'll be perfect for this. After all, you love houses.*

YOU SEEM DETERMINED

If any of you reading this book are parents you will more easily understand this feeling of determination than some others. Remember back to when your child was just beginning to stand and take a few steps on their own. Nothing would deter them from the goal at hand. The average child stands and falls more than 400 times before they can walk. They stand with the assistance of a table or chair, venture out on one foot and boom, down they go. Time and time again, up–down, up-down. They are determined! Do you have that fortitude? Will anything stand in your way of success? Will the lack of income make you forget the goal? I certainly hope not. After all, you've thought this through. You have enough money in your account to make rent or mortgage payments and your credit card has a sizeable unused limit awaiting this lifestyle change. Go for it.........never look back.

The going may get a little rough, but keep believing. You've made an informed decision. Informed? Of course, you're informed. You went to the Career Seminars, didn't you? You asked questions of the people you've interviewed with, haven't you? You took copious notes when you last worked with a Realtor while looking at homes, didn't you? If you honestly answered **no** to any of these suppositions you can keep reading, but you need to do some homework.

Find the local directory and look up Real Estate Agency. Drive around your neighborhood and list the various signs you see in the lawns. Does one company have the majority of those For Sale signs? Do these signs all say For Sale or do some say Under Contract/Pending/Sold? Now go back to the list of agencies and make a few calls. Try to set an appointment with the Office Manager to interview for a place on their team. Depending on the company you choose, the process can take several weeks and many, many interviews, or an hour, one interview and a "let's get you a desk" conclusion.

You know the old saying – You only get one chance to make a good impression – well, in this business it's true. The company I am with insists on at least two interviews. When I was initially looking for a firm with which to work, all I did was call on the phone, ask if they were hiring, stop at the office with my license and bam! I was in.

After being in the business for just under a year, the manager of one of the largest companies in my area called me one afternoon and asked if I would like to talk to her about changing affiliations.

You see, I had just sold a listing of one of her agents and he mentioned I had done a good job and perhaps I'd be interested in making a change. Let me be honest. When I received that call, I was so honored and excited I could hardly breathe. I thought, oh my gosh, I must have done something right. I'm good!!

Seven interviews and a personality test later, I was asked to join the company. This particular manager was so impressed on our first meeting, she wanted to see if it would be the same at every meeting. I thought it was frustrating as all getup, but she kept looking for the façade to break. It never did. Eventually, when I asked her what was taking so long – she welcomed me aboard. Guess she was looking for me to force a decision. I gave her ample input and the position was mine.

IT DOESN'T COST MUCH TO GET STARTED

That's an understatement. Getting started in this business is referred to as an investment, and that investment is expensive. An investment of at least several hundred dollars. But wait, just about everyone involved will accept your credit card. See how easy it is?

I digress at this point to show you how things change. In the 80's when I first became a licensed Real Estate Salesperson all you needed was a sponsor and $50.00. This I could handle. The family would never miss fifty bucks. You picked up a small 25 page pamphlet that detailed the how's, why's, do's and don'ts, some simple rules and regulations and a general recap of 5th grade math.

Read the pamphlet. Learn all you need to know. Schedule an appointment to take the licensing exam and GO FORTH YOUNG SALESPERSON – BE ALL THAT YOU CAN BE. SELL ALL THAT YOU CAN SELL...and give 50% of your earned income to your sponsor. (But wait – you'll hear more about that later.)

Ahh yes, that's how it used to be. But nothing ever stays the same. Some things are meant to change. Change is good. We like change.

Today, you still need that sponsor; legally referred to as your Sponsoring Broker. Without the agreement that someone, someplace, in some company is willing to hold your license and allow you to conduct business under their broad umbrella, you cannot join the Association or MLS (Multiple Listing Service) and you need the MLS.

But, let's back up a minute. Before you can take that test to receive your license and before you can be sponsored by a Broker, you must pay upwards of $500.00 for a Salesperson's Licensing Course. The Department of State is regulating who is qualified to obtain a Real Estate Salesperson license (please keep in mind these are the same licensing people who regulate barbers, cosmetologists, and taxi cab drivers). The Department of State (DOS) monitors this pre-licensing course in the hopes that when you finally pass the exam you'll know how to conduct business in a professional and legal fashion.

Ordinarily the most advantageous method of taking this course is through the local Association of Realtors where someday you aspire to be a card carrying member. All the while you are being taught by the cream of the crop in your new profession, repeat the mantra "I'd never want to be a member of an organization that would allow me membership". That holds more truth than you can ever imagine.

While you are being held captive by these instructors, carefully listen between the lines. You cannot read between the lines because a lot of this stuff will never be written down...just listen and learn. There they stand, in front of the class for the next however many hours (each state may vary) of monitored classroom experience introducing the ABC's of Real Estate Sales.

THE A, B, C'S

A gency. Who do you work for? What you are supposed to do for that client - you'll do whatever it takes to get the Seller to sell to the Buyer and the Buyer to buy from the Seller – you'll never get a pay check if you cannot get them to agree.

B uyers. Find some. Without a Buyer you're like a taxi cab driver with no vehicle. After all, you need someone to show the homes to and meet you for lunch.

C omissions. Another name for paycheck. Remember, you'll need B in order to get to C.

D isclosures. Tell everyone what you know. Find out what you don't know then share that information with everybody involved.

E ducation. You will really get one working in real estate sales. You'll learn the nuts and bolts and then some. When you're new, you're a sponge. Use this opportunity to learn as much as you can - but remember – we learn something new everyday because seldom will a day repeat itself.

F iduciary Duties. Really not as bad as it sounds, and no you don't have to mention it during your weekly confessional. Treat everyone fairly and you'll be just fine.

G uilt. What you experience when you miss your sons guitar solo because you're showing rentals to an out of towner who may after 6 months purchase a very expensive home.

H ome Inspection. A Home Inspection protects the buyer and gives you another opportunity to sell the home a second time to the same people. You see, now they know what's wrong with the property and are unsure of the offer they wrote days before. Fickle aren't they??

I nterest rates. If they're low – that's good. If they're high – that's bad. If they're adjustable – that's food for thought and if they jump – you'd better hope you have money in the bank to keep you in groceries.

J ust ask. Keep talking, ask loads of questions. It's the only way you will learn about people and what they like and dislike. Once you ask, listen to the responses. Stop talking and listen.

K ey access. Keys to homes are locked inside a lockbox on a doorknob of a front door not under a flower pot or doormat. You will use any of several methods to gain entry to this lockbox (keypad, smart phone, but, never a screwdriver).

L ockbox. One of our tools (see above) that makes the job that much easier.

M oney. They have it and we want them to spend it. The more the better. Purchases should be huge. Our commissions should be too.

N eighborhood. Know yours. Make certain your neighbors know you and know what you do as a "profession" or as a "hobby" as the case may be. You do not want to see your competitors sign on your next door neighbor's front lawn.

O pen house. This is your opportunity to meet other agents and feed them lunch. We refer to this as tour or caravan. Additionally we do an open house for the general public. Some old-time agents refer to this as a waste of an afternoon. I always found them to be a great way to meet people who you have a chance to impress with your openness, professionalism and intelligence.

P hone. You cannot be without it. Get a phone that will enable you to text, take pictures, email, open your lockboxes, store all your friends' names and numbers, and tie your shoelaces. Make certain the plan you have is cost efficient. Never be without your phone. If it has a GPS included, even better. You will never want to get separated from your phone.

Q ualify. Buyers must qualify for a mortgage or you will not be considered a Realtor – you'll be a tour guide. Have a favorite mortgage consultant or a list of many you can trust. Have them on speed dial if necessary. Get that Buyer on the phone or at their office ASAP. If they cannot qualify, they cannot buy.

R eady, willing and able. It's not rocket science – find someone who is capable of purchasing a home and has found the home of their dreams. Now run to your car and get the paperwork to draw up a contract.

S igns. A great way to get the phone to ring. Your Broker wants the phone to ring. Put a name rider on your signs or use a hotline number to capture interested callers. Make the yard sign work for you. You may want to add a brochure (info) box.

T axes. You must pay them. Quarterly payments are best to avoid any penalties. Keep records. Keep your receipts. The keyword with taxes is deductions. Maximize them to minimize your tax liability.

U sary. This is a definite no-no. Hardly a problem in our market so all you need to know is it has to do with unusually high interest rates as it pertains to local lending customs.

V inyl siding. This exterior building material is only one of several you will come upon during your listing/selling career. There is a saying in our business with regard to the interior wall finishes in a home, "If you

11

cannot paint it – wallpaper it. If you cannot wallpaper it – panel it. If you cannot panel it – burn it down." With the exception of a newly constructed home, vinyl siding is synonymous to wallpaper. Generally what you find beneath the siding (on an older resale property) is an ugly paint peeling exterior.

W ater. Well or public. Connected or at the street. You will need to know which and if it's a well, find out where it is located and its depth. Is it clean? Can you smell it? Do your job.

X Sign at the x, initial at the x, and always drive slowly at the x walk.

Y ard sales. Watch for them in your neighborhood, they can be a good signal someone is planning to move. Selling baby things? Maybe they'll need another bedroom. Selling furniture? Just maybe they are thinking of downsizing. Be a good neighborhood resource.

Z illo/Zestimates. Sellers and Buyers alike enjoy researching the "value" of a home based on information gathered by an out of the area internet based company. They are not REALTORS and they do not sell properties – but they know(?) the value of your home.

So, now you know the a,b,c's but there is more.

5TH GRADE MATH

Once you have been introduced to, read all about, and taken the tests, you're ready for 5th grade math.

5th grade.....whoa. I can still close my eyes and see the crew cuts, button down collar oxford shirts and white sweat sox that my friends all seemed to be wearing. The girls, of course, had page boy haircuts, knee sox and cardigan sweaters. My math teacher, Mr. Gray spent hours and hours espousing the need for us to know percentages and how to calculate them. (He had to be clairvoyant.) As we got older and moved from our parental homes, we got our first taste of "making ends meet". We finally knew the meaning of percentages... SALES!!!

Women, most but not all, have no problem calculating, in seconds, the cost of a sweater being sold for 40% off the retail price. On the same level, ask a guy to calculate how many miles he can get to a gallon of gas or how far it is to the nearest hardware store in linear feet. We are math geniuses.

Thank you Mr. Gray – with this handful of knowledge I can almost immediately compute 6% of $90,000 less a 5% company marketing fee divided 50/50. That is my check. (less 28% for taxes. Instinctively, I have a harder time with this calculation and payment.)

But once again I digress and we really do need to keep on topic. What will I spend to get started? (Every state varies.)

- ✓ Pre-licensing course $500.
- ✓ License application $50.
- ✓ Association dues $450.
- ✓ MLS service fee $500.

- ✓ Business cards $30.
- ✓ Names riders $50.
- ✓ Office supplies $150.
- ✓ Mont Blanc pen (look successful) $225.
- ✓ Lap top Computer $500.
- ✓ Do everything cell phone (per mo) $150.
- ✓ Lexus $70,000.

So in order to get started and to look successful, you'll need $72,605.

Ok, ok, ok, you can truly look like you're ready for business for just under $2700.

May sound like a fortune, but think about it. Where can you go where you can open your own business with a great reputation and proven business model for a lower personal investment?

DRESS FOR SUCCESS

For the gentlemen reading this book, the standard uniform will be jacket, tie, slacks and leather shoes. Ladies, omit the tie, but don't be surprised if you're expected to wear business suits, hose and heels.

As they say in parts of our country, "Fuggettaboutit." Long gone are the days when we needed to look like a district attorney to show/sell a house. I like to follow one rule – dress for your clientele. If you are working a beach resort – wear a thong! You'll be a multi-million dollar success in no time.

Gents with the washboard abs and a great tan – Italian bikinis will do the trick.

Ski resorts – try a parka and Eskimo boots.

Selling in the desert – use an umbrella for shade and show tents on camelback.

Island properties – learn to swim and sail. But for the majority who live and work in Anytown, USA – you need to look clean, neat, and comfortable.

Do not look better than your clientele. It is not easy for Mr and Mrs Cantmakeendsmeet to sit at the not-yet-paid-for dining table discussing how they can keep from losing the home of their dreams, that they've been unable to make payments on for the last 3 months, ever since Mr lost his job at the refinery and the little woman, who only worked 20 hours a week at the Big K, to see you with a Rolex watch and gold jewelry that probably cost more than their last year's W2's..combined.

Make the client comfortable. Become a chameleon. For the 60 minutes or so you have to sit at that not-yet-paid-for dining table, become a friend...or at least someone they would want to spend some time with. If they are jealous and hate you, forget about ever gaining their trust. That listing will have another more likable and less snooty agents sign in the lawn.

On the other hand, I've always liked the idea that Buyers enjoy riding around in a car they will never be able to own. Agents driving Neons and Saturns may have the common man/woman aura, yet the Buyers who are looking at $50,000 starter homes deserve some part of the dream. But then again, does the executive referred to you by Out-of-Town Realty Inc. really want to ride around looking for a home in a cramped 2 door sedan that is smaller than the car they drove in high school? I think not. This can be a dilemma. Maybe you can borrow your teenager's car when needed. Just make sure it's clean.

WHAT'S IN YOUR TRUNK?

At this point it is understood you need to dress for your clientele – business, business-casual, cool dude-ish, a bathing suit and flip-flops – but, just as important as your look --- is your equipment. Have you got what it takes?

Smart phone, computer, lock box access, measuring device, flag markers, corner signs, nuts and bolts, and procedural manuals, to name only a portion of your personal arsenal.

You can put your office in your car or you can leave the house/office empty handed. I never like to be caught off guard. If I need a purchase contract after showing a home – I can pull one out of my trunk and take the buyer to Starbucks to sign. If I'm putting information sheets inside a brochure box on the for sale sign and the box falls off in my hand –I have a screwdriver, screws, nuts and bolts or duck tape to repair it. Finally getting your buyers to look at a crappy foreclosure property down the street at dusk – I have a flashlight to lead the way.

Some of my friends bring all of this into the home with them – they look like they are about to board an outgoing flight with the weekender packed for a three day stay. They are ready for anything. I'm ready for it all, except I have found it a lot easier and less intrusive to leave the luggage in the car.

Ever considered having a pair of boots in your car? Mud can ruin a good pair of Manolas. I prefer to call them my "muck shoes" and you'll need a pair. Choose one in a crazy color so everyone will know you would never actually wear them if you didn't have good reason.

Here are a few essentials most agents never think of having at their disposal:

Toothpaste, for example. Can you figure why you need this one? I'm not talking fresh and clean mouth toothpaste. I'm talking about toothpaste to fill nail holes.

Great story: Several years ago I was selling a lovely home for an older couple. A week before closing, I visited them and noticed they had over a hundred nail holes from where they had removed photos and artwork. I mentioned they could use toothpaste to fill in the holes rather than go out and purchase spackle. A small dab on the end of your finger works wonders. When we finally closed on the sale one week later, I met the buyers and they were confused. They mentioned to me that strangely every wall in the house was covered with green dots. Did I know anything about it? Hmmm, that made me think – next time be certain to tell the seller to use WHITE toothpaste – not that green, minty, fluoride stuff!!

WD-40 is terrific. Works to lubricate door hinges, keys turn easier, and it gets gum out of your hair. Keep it around. Makes life a lot easier.

Cat litter sprinkled under your tires will give you instant traction on snow and ice. Also works great to sop up vomit when it appears on your car seat or floor mats thanks to a car sick child in the back seat.

The throw rug – you already know why. Put it at the front entry way of any home you are having open and you will not have the mess you would have otherwise. Living in central New York has forced Realtors to be creative. We have frozen locks, iced driveways, and messy floors.

Hand sanitizer – put it in a blow-up pool and bathe in it after a listing appointment or showing of a not-so-clean home. Another true story: I was called by a friend of a friend who lived out of state to go list a home that had been rented for the past three years. The tenants were moving and the house was to be sold. I went over

18

at the appointed time and was met by a very pregnant woman, holding a baby, a toddler on the floor in diapers and 3 dogs. The place was a mess. I dutifully took notes as I generally do and when I was walking up and down the stairs I would have sworn they were moving. I blamed this swaying feeling on a new pair of glasses and kept on with the task at hand. When I left the house, I looked down and noticed I was covered with fleas!! There was such a heavy contamination of those blood sucking creatures, the carpet was moving – moving in waves of undulating bugs. Needless to say, the tenants left and the entire house was cleared of all the floor coverings and fumigated...3 times.

Then, of course, there are the usual items everyone should carry – food and water, an umbrella, a hat, warm sox, a few toys and always a current telephone book. I think these make sense and need little explanation. The telephone book is useful for just about every situation:

- Running late—no phone number—look it up

- Forget the address of the attorney-look it up

- Last minute reservation-look it up

- Call the kids school-look it up

- Need medical attention-look it up

- Client too short to see out the window-instant booster seat!!

Yes, the telephone book has unlimited uses and is helpful to get us out of numerous binds. In Central New York – can't find WD-40 and the car won't start – get the phone book, grab the BIC, start a fire to keep warm and help will be here soon.

HIGH TECH, LOW TECH, NO TECH

Every day you are in the Real Estate business someone will try to sell you something to help you look more successful, something to help you be more successful or to make your life easier. Bottom line: you're in sales. That simply means you should be able to spot a salesman and a gimmick long before the average Joe. This is obvious, right? Not necessarily. Even if you don't own your own laptop (and a lot of new agents don't) when you use the computers in your office, you'll be inundated with special offers for everything from cameras to magnets; calendars to key chains; pens and notepads to vacations.

You should be able to recognize a pitch long before it is delivered. But, truth is – the internet is a magical place. We can email strangers and see homes in far away cities. Your customers know more about the Real Estate market in your town than you do. After all, they have been active on the internet long before you were. You've been taking classes and getting ready to "do business" while they have been shopping and researching data.

Be careful. Take your time. Listen and watch. Is that lap top computer that can plug into the cigarette lighter necessary? Probably, but not right now. Can you show homes and write contracts without a Mont Blanc pen. Of course you can. Use a BIC and make it a gift to the buyer when the process is over.

The surest way to insure your success is to purchase something you cannot afford and be totally responsible for paying for it. Work to make that payment.

When I first got my license I was driving a mid size family four door sedan. Dark gray with cloth interior. Large trunk. That car had it all and I could easily afford the lease payment each month. Hell. It was cheap. It was not motivational!! It did not demand I work hard to keep it.

Nine months of doing what you hope to be doing for the rest of your life, I leased a new car. A pretty car. A car with leather interior and a hood ornament. A car with European heritage. A car that said, "I am successful". A car I had to pay for – and work to support.

Today just about everyone uses their cell phone to keep track of daily appointments. We look busy. We are busy. We had better be busy. If not, we are idiots. Technology can make your life easier or it can make your life a living hell. You have two choices with technology. If you choose to embrace it, you'd better understand it. Take the necessary courses (your local real estate association probably holds classes instructing you how to maximize the benefits of being connected). Become informed. If you choose to ignore technology, find someone to do it for you. One way or another you cannot be a success if you keep your head in the sand. First graders can be rather helpful here – they are not as judgmental as the computer nerds and they have great games!

GETTING PAID FOR WHAT YOU DO

Commissions. You will not be paid weekly, bi-weekly, or monthly in this business. Checks come to you when you close a transaction and the Seller, or the Buyer, pays your fee.

Most companies will start a new agent out at a 50/50 split. You do all of the work. They let you use their telephone, desk, forms, computer, and parking lot. This symbiotic relationship has been on-going since the first caveman took possession of the dream cave and moved his family into the new digs. The go-between who brokered the deal (currently referred to as an agent working under the Broker's umbrella) was paid in clam shells and tiger hides. When the agent reported back to the office that Gronk and his family were happy and gave him shells and tiger hides in appreciation, the leader claimed his equal share. After all, he was the person with whom this agent had asked questions and from whom the sage advice had arisen. The more people this illustrious leader has looking for relocating cavemen and their families the better---more shells and tiger hides to share.

As the more aggressive agents become successful the leader realizes he must take less and less from these "stars". It is therefore an age old dilemma – attract them, teach them, then pay up or lose them to the other boss who will pay more. Pity we are so hell bent on all things monetary.

PAPERWORK, POLICIES OR PROCEDURES

It can be the policy of your company, or a best practice you've been told not to deviate from, or a procedure you think keeps you on tract; no matter what you call it everyone will want you to follow it and nobody who is highly successful ever sees the reason why.

"There are too many rules and it cramps my style. I'm successful doing it this way, why do I have to change?"

"Why can't I get any help? Can I hire someone to help me?"

"I gave you everything I had, why do you continue to ask?"

"No I did not get everyone's signature on that page. Why do you need it?"

"Could anyone make copies of this for me?"

"I want to write an ad for an open house. Can I do it on this paper? Why do I need a form?"

"These buyers only want to see if they can pay $150,000 on a house listed for $225,000 – why do I need to write it down?"

"The attorney wants me to get this signed by the Seller – can I sign it instead?"

"If everyone has to initial this change, I'll need to call them all and have them meet with me. I did not like them the first time and honestly, I never wanted to see them again. Can you just do it?"

"Can I hold this deposit check till I get paid and cash it then? What do you mean it's not mine? They gave it to me."

"I'm at an open house and I'm bored. Can I go now?"

"These people are making me nuts. Is it okay if I just drive away really fast when we arrive at the next appointment? They'll make it home."

"As long as the Seller is home, you don't need me. Just go over and introduce yourselves. Call me if you want to buy it."

"Why can't we use the toilet in this house?"

"This freshly baked cake smells and looks great. It's probably for us, don't you think? Can we have some?"

"What smells?"

"The Seller just called my manager. They think I'm doing a lousy job. Okay. Can you handle them from now on? They liked talking to you."

"Can I charge the buyers $5 per home I show them? Too little? Too much? Why not? I'm not getting paid by the hour."

"My kid really likes the pool and it's so hot — is it okay if we swim for a few minutes? Leave us here and come back in an hour."

At one time or another, we have heard every one of these comments and we have allowed each one to gestate in our minds. We love people. We love homes. We love the challenge. We love the process. Cripe! Is there anything about being a Realtor we don't love?

YES. The whining, selfish, dirty, stinky, work without pay, chauffeuring and hand-holding that we do every day? Maybe. It could be worse though. We could be with the same people 8 hours a day - day in and day out. We're not. Generally, we spend less than 90 days with any given buyer or seller. Seems like a lifetime.

FINDING A SELLER WHO NEEDS YOU

Oh! Happy Day! You've got a listing appointment. How it happened is probably a mystery and I am certain the excitement is keeping you awake at night. Like the Boy Scout rules – Be Prepared....and be on time. This is your first impression. Here's your chance to wow them. Don't be late because you got lost. Scope out the area, house, schools, and shopping prior to the appointment. If you've never been to this side of town before – learn it. You cannot show up at the Sellers door looking like you needed a map to get there. After all you are responsible for getting the traffic here in hopes of finding a buyer.

When you meet the Seller, be confident and upbeat. You may have noticed peeling paint at the entry, detected a faint smell of cat urine as you entered, and been accosted by the family dog before taking off your shoes. (By all means, do remove your shoes. These lovely people do not live in a hovel. Every homeowner knows their home is a castle.) They want you to be thrilled that you were invited to this party.

If necessary, practice being pleasant if meeting new people in unfamiliar surroundings gives you hives. It is unfortunate this needs to be said but, in our world today, both men and women need to be careful walking into homes occupied by strangers. Men have been accused of inappropriate activity even though they were met at the front door by a very attractive lady who at 2:00 in the afternoon has not had a chance to get dressed.

Women have been accosted by men who met them at the door, invited them inside, and then pretended to have important information in another room. Instances have been reported where everything was going smoothly until the agent and homeowner reached the bedroom area. Then all hell broke loose. The homeowner was attacked and sexually assaulted. (Perhaps it was the other way around, I can't recall.)

The odds of anything ever happening to you or to anyone you know are probably less than one in 5000, but it does happen. You need to be careful and use common sense. Keep your cell phone in your pocket. Let another person know where you are going and at what time you should be finished. You can let your office secretary know where you'll be and she can call you at a predetermined time. No answer? Call in the National Guard. If you're fine you can share your contingency plan with the client and have a laugh about your paranoia.

You need to gather information from these people as to their motivation (why are they moving). Is it a job change, divorce, a baby on the way, empty nesters, down-sizing, upgrading, mother-in-law moving in or is she finally moving out? What is their time frame? Do they have all the time in the world or has one partner already begun a new job in a new location? Listen with interest even if you must pretend to care about them. Their lives are in upheaval now and they've asked you to guide them through this life change.

Politely ask if you can have a tour of their home. Take notes. You'll never remember all of the details when you get back to the office. I usually bring all of my listing information in a manila folder and use the back for notes. After a while you'll find you follow the same pattern each time you preview a property. Foyer to living room dining room, kitchen to family room on the first floor. Then upstairs to the bedrooms and baths. (It's a good idea to follow this same path when you show homes.) Going from main level to second floor is only one flight of stairs, if you go from the main level to the basement and then to the upper floor you may be too winded to ask questions when you finally get to the attic/crawlspace. Pace yourself. The basement and garage are generally dirty and if so, the Seller may suggest you put your shoes back on. Be your own judge. Slip on shoes are easy – wear them always – shoes that tie are a pain in your back. Tying and untying will eventually wear you down and spoil your day.

Be prepared. Bring some data with you. Have the basic information from the tax records. What did they pay for the property? What is the assessed value? Which school will the kids attend? Have your business card and propaganda about you and your firm.

Explain clearly how it would be impossible for you to offer an opinion of list pricing this minute. You've never seen the interior of their home before. You are familiar with the area and fully confident the home will sell in today's market but it would be unfair of you to suggest a price now. You must do your homework. You'll need to compare this "castle" to the other homes in the 'kingdom". (At this point they will usually let you know that they have been in every home on their street and theirs is the largest, nicest and most expensive. This is ordinarily not the case, but listen and buy yourself time to get the figures right.)

Additionally, this Seller just gave you a vital piece of information that you might have missed. He's an arrogant know it all. Be careful. He will need special handling. Any information you give him must be substantiated by facts not instinct. Handle him with platitudes and he'll list with a competitor. Professionalism and experience will win him over. If you're short on experience, know your stuff.

Thank him, return to your office, notes in hand, access your computer and begin your Comparative Market Analysis (CMA). Some agents will refer to this process as a Competitive Market Analysis and they will focus on the homes that will be competing with your subject property for a small number of buyers. Don't let this make you a nervous wreck. You gather the data and interpret the findings. The numbers are the numbers. It's the delivery that will make or break your career. Therefore, learn the best way to deliver your message.

BUILDING THE C.M.A.

The CMA is a tool used for generations by Realtors who hope to accurately price properties. More appropriately, the CMA is an acronym for COVER MY ASSETS, because this is exactly what you hope to do.

Look at all of the homes of similar style, size, and amenities in any given area surrounding your subject property. Compare these available properties with some that have sold recently. You should work to get really good at doing these exercises. The knowledge will serve you well. After years of completing each CMA as if you were doing it for your high school math symposium – you'll do them in your sleep.

There is one small caveat that should be addressed at this point....Accuracy. Try not to fall prey to the CMA being created to reflect a lower or higher than recommended price. You'll live to regret it. If all of the homes in this subject area have been listed/sold for $135,000 don't price this home at $175,000 just because the Seller thinks he can get it. The only one getting it is you... you're getting hosed!!

Be professional. Just because the patient (Seller) doesn't want to hear the bad news from the doctor (you) does not mean he won't eventually hear the truth....cancer. 6 weeks to live(your home is really no better, perhaps even a little bit worse, than your neighbor and only worth $120,000). Feeling sorry for them will not change the facts. The difference is in the delivery. You are either the doctor with excellent bedside manners or the jerk who bluntly tells you the problem. The jerk may be a great doctor but nine times out of ten, his referral business will be nothing to brag about.

It would not be even remotely interesting to tell you how to complete a CMA here. I would put you to sleep in no time. Let your office manager or training person bore you. Not me. I merely want you to know what it is, when we do them and why it's important. You've heard the what – here's the when. A CMA is used to establish a list price when offering a home for sale. Conversely you'll offer to do a CMA for the Buyer who wants to know he is not overpaying for a cardboard, 2 bedroom, 1 bath, 400 sq. ft home in the middle of a flood zone just because it is close to his gym.

Why is it important? It's the first step to evaluating the property. When the home eventually sells, if the lender (bank)is involved, they will insist on an appraisal. Is the home worth the amount of money they are willing to lend you? If not, forget it. You won't get the mortgage and the sale will not finalize.

If you do accurate homework in the beginning you never run the risk of losing your financing at the last minute. Lose your financing – lose your buyer. You will not get paid. You will not be able to pay for the expensive car you leased. No vacations. Do it right the first time.

FARMING...and I don't mean crops

Remember when you told your family you'd have no trouble finding people to work with? It was going to be easy. After all you've lived in this town forever. Went to grammar and high school here. You bagged groceries at the local market. You babysat for half the kids in town. Funny thing is – now you're entering the Real Estate industry. Those people you knew have already bought a home. They know someone in the business. You weren't there when they needed someone and since then they've met a wonderful caring individual who still sends them a card every year in hopes of continuing to be their best friend and the only person thought about when it comes to sell that home and buy another. They will always remember the fun times had by one and all during the house hunting process. As you will come to realize, this is a special bond... a very special relationship. It is a relationship you will covet for years to come and a relationship that other agents will work hard to maintain.

Find new victims – I mean strangers, to work with. Get your name out there. Sit in other agents open houses. Walk door to door with business cards. Send out flyers. Offer to take floor time (also referred to by your broker as opportunity time.) You may get someone if you work in an office that has heavy traffic. If you work in an office on the 11th floor of a high rise office building – people may not hop on the elevator to see you if they can drive to a free standing office and walk in the front door. Nonetheless, be prepared. Be ready to answer questions. Don't be afraid to ask for business. When you are at a party and people start talking about interest rates or what the house on the corner of First and Main sold for...know the answers. Try to be the 'go-to guy'. If they need information, go to the right place to get it. If you become a resource of information and share this information freely – eventually someone will tell a friend or a neighbor about you. Your name will get around, and that's a very good thing.

If you are uncomfortable approaching a total stranger, share these feelings with your broker. Then ask for a job at the front reception desk. At least you'll get a check every week and you can still say you work in the real estate industry.

HOLY COW....YOU FINALLY GOT ONE

Somebody called and asked for you....by name. A real life referral from your next door neighbors brother in law. Their son just got married and at the reception they told the happy couple to call you. Good God---now you've arrived. You are amongst the thousands of Real Estate agents with a Buyer. The excitement may be too much. Not to mention the unbridled fear.

- Where do they want to live?

- How much can they spend?

- When do they want to move in?

- Do I really think I'm qualified to help anyone buy the largest investment of their young married life?

- Is my car clean?

Breathe---slowly and deeply. This is not rocket science. (If it were, you wouldn't be interested in doing it, would you?)

Make an appointment to meet with them. Plan to ask them questions. Find out as much as you can. You're not being nosy, just doing your job. Have they been to a mortgage consultant yet? If not, get them to one as soon as possible. You need to know if they really can buy a home when they find the one of their dreams. Let's recall what I told you about the doctor – does he really care that you had your tonsils out at age 8, your appendix at age 21 and began losing your hair at 40? No, but if he finds out you have a rare blood disorder he will remember it. And some day it will be important. So will the bankruptcy, the judgments, and the student loans.

During this interview process, those innocent, yet nosy questions will give you gobs of information. Use it to your benefit. Determine what they need. They just got married. Do they plan on a family? Will they need an extra bedroom for family that will come to visit? Do they have student loans to pay every month? How many jobs have they had in the past three years? Do they have any money saved? Do the parents have any money to give them? Find out. You need to know and they need to know that you need to know. Know what I mean????

OK. Let's assume all is fine in buyer-land and they actually can afford a place to call home. Search your computer programs and find them their dream home. Search morning, noon and night. After all what else do you have to do – you're a newbie!!

You may end up with only one or as many as eighty-seven homes that match most of the specifications on their wish list. Put them in your car and get going. You are about to show properties. (Isn't this what it's all about?)

LET'S LOOK AT A FEW HOUSES

Finally you've located a Buyer and have researched their needs successfully finding a few homes that match the criteria. Thursday night you'll meet at the office, climb into your car and begin the 3 hour tour.

Whoa. Don't get ahead of yourself. First you have to make the appointments. The showing instructions for each listing are spelled out in the MLS printout. Do you have to call the listing agent or the seller to make arrangements? Follow the instructions. Perhaps the property has a lockbox on the door and all you need to do is call and leave a message as to the time you will be there. If this is the case, make certain you have a full battery in your access pad or your phone is charged so you can actually access the key.

Beware of telling anyone you will be at the home at a specific time. If you run into car problems, if the Buyer takes longer than you expected at house number one, your schedule will be off all evening. Use a range of time – between 5 and 6, 4:30 and 6. Be the professional but always make time for surprises.

Map out your plan of attack. Have copies of the information sheets for each home available for the Buyer. Let the Buyer look over the information and give them a pen so they can take notes if they want. You are the leader, they need to follow. And remember, this is fun. YOU LOVE HOUSES!!!

If the Seller is at home, introduce yourself and your Buyers. Remember, selling real estate is an emotional event. If the Seller likes both you and your Buyers, the family may be more likely to think they'll be the perfect addition to the neighborhood and a lower than expected offer may be acceptable. Emotions have a great deal to do with successful negotiations.

Show the first floor then the second – I told you earlier – any other plan of attack may leave you too tired to go from cellar to attic in every home.

Additionally, if your Buyer hates the first floor layout, seeing the basement will not matter. Save your energy for when it counts. Make your thank yous, leave your card, and move on.

Did they sign a Buyer Agency Contract? I hope so. In many of the 50 states, we have the ability to represent Buyers in these transactions as well as Sellers. Explain why they may want an advocate to represent them. Go through the form and make certain they understand it. Once they have a copy, proceed with the activities!

OH MY GOSH...THEY BROUGHT SAM AND LIZZY

Your worst nightmare. The Buyer could not get a sitter so you'll be driving around with a 4 and 6 year old in the back seat. Worse yet, Mom brought crayons and juice boxes to keep them happy. Dad has a bag of gummy bears and chips. Don't get me wrong – I love kids. I have 2 and 4 grandchildren, and I have lived with the remnants of food, drink and writing material in the back seat of my rather expensive, European made car with a fancy hood ornament. But not when Dad and Mom had buying a house in three days weighing heavily on their minds. Simply put no one is watching the kids!

Someone has to step up. Guess who? That would be me. When Mom and Dad are looking at the house, I'm talking to the kids. While Mom and Dad are rearranging the furniture, I'm watching the kids. While Mom and Dad are asking the "buying" questions I had hoped to hear – I'm watching the kids.

What's more important? I honestly don't know. If the house is meant for them – nothing I say will change it, but I can help them make a decision by allowing them some uninterrupted time to imagine their family living within these four walls.

I am doing my job. They will thank me. They will remember how I kept the kids entertained, fed and happy so they could look at potential properties. I didn't have a lot of control when I was driving so they did eat a lot of garbage and there were some crayon marks on the leather seats – so what. Some 409 removed it and this family will be my client forever. As a matter of fact, there is a photo of all of us on their fridge. Can't beat that!

NAKED TENANTS

Now here is a topic I can wrap my arms around. This is a reality. I've shown properties where the homeowner had a life size nude self-portrait on the landing. Another had the two men posed in a very compromising manner. Upon closer look (and I hope I was not caught looking closer) I realized one of them was no other than the owner who was showing me the townhouse!

Once I was showing a home to a nice guy about 27 years old. The Seller, a woman about 55 offered to leave a naked portrait of herself if he wanted it. He politely responded, "No thank you."

You'll always be surprised when this happens and you cannot prepare yourself for it. Avert your eyes, try not to blush and move on to another room.

I remember one time I rang the doorbell and a young fellow answered the door wrapped in a towel. He let us in and disappeared. We toured the main floor and upon entering the second floor found our gentleman in one of the bedrooms – not alone – and very disinterested in us being there. He was otherwise involved. The girl didn't seem to mind our presence either. I can safely say we did not take the time to look in the closet and measure the floor space.

THERE'S AN OPEN HOUSE

We all do them. Love 'em or hate 'em – an open house is a necessary part of our business. In my area we do the majority of them on Sunday afternoons, but you may prefer Thursday evenings, Saturday mornings, or any day of the week from sun up to sun set. Plan to schedule the open house for the surroundings and the area.

There are tricks to having a successful open house. Is your listing near a church? Make certain your open house hours coincide with the end of church services. Are you near a school where the monthly PTA meets on Thursdays @ 7:30? Perhaps you should plan an evening open house. Does the local commuter train pass by every day @ 6:45 am and again @ 6:45 pm? Times to avoid. I think you're beginning to get the idea. Use the open house to your advantage. Schedule them to attract maximum attention. Be prepared for the public, the weather, and that rare instance when other agents will send their buyers to view your inventory.

A Buyer who is working with another agent can be wasting your time or searching on their own. Your buyer may do the same. This is how and where an open house can get ugly.

Think about this scenario: The buyer you worked with all day Friday and Saturday decides you need a day off or maybe you're just too busy to put aside several hours on the following Sunday. They are just going to drive around looking at homes to see if any of them look interesting. If they see anything they like, they'll call you. CAREFUL. You have just set up the scenario whereas these buyers will fall in love. The law of averages works like this – if you had taken them to see this particular home, they would have hemmed and hawed and ended up placing this so-so house on their short list. Because they are without you and at the mercy of the agent holding the open house, who tells them it is a hot house, several other buyers have expressed interest, and if they don't move quickly they may lose it – and they found it on their own – they want it before anyone else can beat them to it.

Herein enters the dilemma. Do they call you to meet them and write a contract or are they so excited they forget all about you and use the nice old lady holding the house open? Depends. Have you told them to show your card when they walk in? Did they tell the lovely old lady they were working with you? Did you not have this discussion with them because they should know the rules? They may have agreed but can no longer recall the conversation. When that emotion of falling in love kicks them in the gut all they know is they want it. If you are involved it will be because you have a great relationship with the other agent or your buyers protected you. Possible, but doesn't happen often.

You should take measures to protect yourself and your well earned fee by explaining how you work and how they need to act. You should work with an Exclusive Buyer Agent contract (if they are available in your state) whereas the Buyer signs an agreement (similar to having a seller sign a listing contract) to be represented solely by you and your firm for a definitive period of time. Each side has well defined responsibilities – loyalty and diligence among them. Talk about this with the buyer and your value will become very clear. They will appreciate the fact that they are unequivocally represented. You will act as their advocate throughout the process.

SHOWING PROPERTIES

Finally, you're doing exactly what you always thought Realtors did. Looking at those homes you said you loved so much. WRONG. Successful Realtors do not show property. They sell property.

If there are more than 10 homes that match your clients preferences, narrow it down. Perhaps you can ask them to take a drive by all 87 homes matching their wish list and they can narrow it down to a manageable few. Re-examine the wish list. Prioritize. If you spend all day, every day showing them all 87 homes – they will be so confused you'll need to do it all over again just to eliminate the junk. Now it's not just 87 homes --- it's 174 homes. If you're not careful it could be 348 in no time!! (87 x 2; 174 x 2... more 5th grade math)

STOP. Go back to the initial interview. Ask a few more questions. This will save you time and energy.

Of course you understand that when they do find their dream home, they will not want to pay the asking price. It has to be negotiated. Just because the home is listed for $82,500 does not mean it is worth $82,500. (Keep in mind, you have shown them everything else they narrowed down in the same price range and this is the best choice for the money.) All of the homes in this area, of similar style and size have sold between $81,000 and $84,000 but it still means nothing. They want to offer $73,000 because that's what Uncle Harry said to do. Come in low. You can always go up.

If you become a skilled negotiator, this is where the fun begins. Anybody can write a full price offer; only the best can successfully negotiate a low-ball offer. Look at it this way, you're only Nine thousand five hundred dollars apart. If you split the difference each side would be sacrificing $4,250.

{adjusted offer $73,000 + 4,250 = $77,250}

{list price of $82,500 − 4,250 = $77,250}

That offer will probably not reflect the Sellers opinion of fair market value nonetheless. The lowest sale in the area was $81,000.

Ask yourself a few questions...

- Is this house equal to that lowest sale in amenities?

- How does the condition compare?

- Is the location as desirable, or more so?

Adjust and instruct. Help them to see the light. Use common sense. Use emotion. Recognize each party wants to walk away a winner. The newlyweds want to get the bargain Uncle Harry said they should get and the Seller wants to save face and pay his expenses. Can this be negotiated?? Probably not. Why?? You did not do your job well enough to counteract Uncle Harry's words of advice. Now, be the professional and coach them on how this should be done. Find a fair priced home with the amenities they want, in the location they prefer and let them know they have to PAY FOR IT. Remember the CMA you read about earlier? Put it to good use. Counsel them. If Uncle Harry is going to be in on every discussion – by golly, put him in the car with the kids. He should get a good look at the garbage that is out there so that when a great house comes along his advice will not stand in the way.

Some areas have one more Uncle Harry that will become a party to this transaction. We call them Home Inspectors. Most are wonderful men and women. A joy to have as an integral part of any home buying experience. Others are horrid. They are consumed with some sense of pseudo power or fear, I don't know which. Powerful to the point that he/she will let you know they could have built (or maintained) this home better than anyone else-or- fear that they will miss something and you will hold them responsible.

Rely on your colleagues. They will give you a list of qualified inspectors they have faith in. Call them and accompany the inspector at the job. You will learn more during one 3 hour inspection than any course can teach you. The good guys know their stuff and are worth every penny they are paid.

Once each party has agreed on a sale price and the inspection has been completed, get these cute kids to a lender to complete a mortgage application.

There should be no surprises here. You asked all the right questions and you had them pre-approved prior to writing the initial offer. Now is when you find out they "forgot" the judgment and subsequent bankruptcy four years ago, and until only recently they were guests of a federal B&B (state prison). Overlook the fact that they spent all of their down payment money on the slots during their honeymoon. Be resourceful. Find a relative who will give them a gift letter for the down payment. The judgment and bankruptcy can be glossed over if some length of time has passed and the kids will agree to pay (and qualify for) a higher interest rate. There must be a federally subsidized mortgage program out there someplace that will help parolees buy a home – after all that's fair, isn't it? Guess you learned another lesson...we all make mistakes.

NEGOTIATING

Possibly one of the most coveted skills in this industry. A great negotiator can perform miracles. A Buyer and Seller can begin the process miles apart and yet arrive at an amicable agreement with the help of a skilled negotiator. The key to success is to remember – you are part of the solution not a part of the problem.

The way you deliver the message can mean success or failure. Keeping the larger picture in mind rather than a lot of little pieces paves the road to an agreement.

Successful negotiators have the people skills necessary to make things happen. They are either born with them or acquire the skills as they grow and mature. When emotions are running high – which happens when we fall in love, buy that first home, move to a country where we do not speak the language, have a child, downsize because the kids have left home – our common sense takes a back seat to our emotions.

A good negotiator lets the Buyer know the Seller was very happy to receive an offer (there is no need to ever let them know they would never accept such a low-ball offer, leave the washer and dryer behind and vacate in 10 days) but are unable to accept the price. If the Buyer would consider ___, they can have the washer and dryer and close in 30 days. This is a positive communication and no speed bumps appear on the road ahead.

The agent who takes the Sellers response back to the Buyer word for ugly disappointed word will usually fail. Perhaps what we need is TACT. Some of us are just more tactful than others. If this bull in the china shop describes you – learn from your peers. Who in your sphere is always the person who gets results? Is anyone especially good at getting everything their way? Are they successful in getting prices reduced? Do they always get extensions if necessary?

These agents are great negotiators. They have the skills you need. Ask for advice. Listen to them when they are negotiating contracts. One thing I said before and it is a good place to build a foundation for future negotiations – be part of the solution, not part of the problem.

OMG! THEY SAID YES

Even more exciting than negotiating a low-ball offer is the moment the seller says YES. I'll take it. Where should I sign?

A paycheck is within your grasp after many hours of hard work and training classes. What happens next?

If your Buyer/Seller does not have an attorney, ask your colleagues for the name of a Realtor friendly real estate attorney. You are not looking for anyone who will make poor decisions with regard to the client based on a loyalty to you – you're looking for an attorney who will be fair in his charges, reasonable with expenses, keep the client informed and make certain there will be a check made payable to your firm at the closing table.

This is a real estate friendly attorney.

Get the contract and all of the pertinent addenda to the attorney who will have an opportunity to review it and further discuss what is ahead with the client. There may be inspections involved in your contract. He will want to make certain the client understands these inspections and the possible discussions to be had after the inspections have been completed. Once the attorney and the client are comfortable each understands the process ahead, an attorney approval is the next step.

Home Inspections will be addressed in another chapter, but needless to say, a professional inspector will go through the home with a trained eye looking for any and all problems. They inspect the heating/cooling systems, electrical outlets and boxes, windows, toilets, tubs, sinks and appliances. They will examine the roof and the chimney. When completed, the report can be as many as thirty pages or as few as three. I've seen inspectors leave a home shocked at how poorly it was constructed. They are usually not confused at the construction; they are confused that it is still standing. Other times, the inspector can find nothing to report. (I always told my home sellers that if they have maintained the home and all of the various parts of the home adequately, they have nothing to fear. If they have deferred the everyday normal maintenance of the home, they may have a report with several highlighted areas of concern.) Regardless of the findings, you may have to begin further discussions as to how these 'shortcomings' will be handled.

Let's move on to the next phase of selling a home: financing. Lenders are becoming less lenient and creative than in the past. Since 2009, we have experienced one of the worst housing problems in our nation's history. Not since the Eisenhower administration have we seen unemployment as high and housing sales so delayed. Banks are cracking down on policies that used to allow Buyers to overextend themselves. Find a lender you trust. You will enlist this person (usually referred to as a mortgage consultant or mortgage originator) to help your clients get pre-approved and ultimately financed.

Once all of these small hurdles have passed, you are looking at the ultimate in our careers... a closing and even better the paycheck.

Attend the closing. Put a smile on your face and thank everyone involved for making this the happiest day in these people's lives. Bring a small gift if you wish. Something useful. A bottle of wine, a mailbox or a six pack of flowers to start a garden. Whatever your wallet can allow. It needn't be expensive, but it should be something that will – as long as they live in that home – remind them of you. Your business card made into a magnet is cute, but it should not be the only gift.

Take the commission check back to your office, hand it to whoever is supposed to receive it, and have a drink. The worst is over. You need to do this another hundred and ten times before it gets old and even then, the thrill of helping people change their lives is, in a word, awesome.

BANKS AND THEIR RULES

Mortgage brokers, bankers and internet lenders – every one of them is scrambling for your buyer.

I sold a home once to a buyer with no job. She quit her job and wanted to sell AVON from her home. Good for her. Another entrepreneur in the making. Who am I to stand in her way? Only problem – her timing. She had a job when she started looking for a home. She had a job when she found the home of her dreams and negotiated the contract price. By the time she made her bank application, this girl had an apartment full of lip gloss and skin-so-soft.

As soon as the lender who gave her a pre-approval letter found out there was no job to verify or a recent pay stub to put in the file they pulled her pre-approval. No one will give a mortgage to anyone without verifiable employment and more recently, a FICO score over 625. No one that is except, an internet lender. If you can pay the high rate of interest they charge and the additional points they add to the bottom line, you will get a loan.

My young buyer pursued an internet lender and eventually closed on her new home. Currently she is happily selling AVON products to all of her neighbors in her old apartment complex (where she is currently living). You see she had to sell her home or see it go into foreclosure when she could not make the monthly payments.

I know what you're thinking. Lucky sales agent. I had a new listing. Two commissions from one buyer! Yes, I was paid a commission when I sold her the home originally and again I earned a commission when she had to sell. This young girl may have been able to buy her dream home, but she couldn't keep it. Had she gone the traditional route and waited until she was established in her sales career, this fiasco could have been avoided.

The rules for getting a mortgage have changed drastically in the past year. Everything now is credit score driven. There were times when a Doctor, right out of medical school had a blank check with the bankers. They knew the income of a new doctor could go nowhere but up. If they couldn't afford the payment now, they sure would be able to after a year on the job. Answer? Place these high earners in an adjustable rate loan. Start out at an artificially low rate of interest and in one, three, five, seven or ten years it would readjust. No problem. They'd be partners in the practice by then. Good thinking if it worked. Usually, these up and coming doctors were lured away to a new city and sold those homes.

ATTORNEYS and HOME INSPECTORS

There are times when you will thank your lucky stars either the attorney or the home inspector is in your corner and protecting both the Buyer/Seller and you from a huge potential mistake. Other times you'll want to string them up by their nose hairs.

I've worked with attorneys who will charge their client $250 for a closing and others who charge 1% of the purchase price (that could be $2500 in some cases). Ask up front. Can your buyer afford a $2500 bill?

Home Inspectors love to hear the sound of their own voices. They really need to find some flaws. No house is perfect. It's all in the presentation. Think back to that blind date in high school – being told 'she has a wonderful personality'. Translated that means she's not much to look at but a nice person. Same with homes – they may have good bones but need cosmetic work. Nothing a make-over cannot fix!!

I once sold a home to a young girl and the Home Inspector trashed it from top to bottom. Everything was wrong from the pipes making noise to the heat exchanger in the furnace having a crack. Of course this report scared her and she ran away from her first investment opportunity. A few days later this Home Inspector called to ask if the sale had gone sour. I replied it had and thanked him for protecting my client so well. He was our hero until he asked to purchase the same home!! He said it was a great property and he'd make it work. I thought this guy was honest and trustworthy. Guess not.

Since then, I've found some Home Inspectors I do trust. I've used them to inspect my home, my kids homes and my friends' homes. He takes his job seriously. Find a guy/gal (yes, there are female home inspectors) who is thorough, conscientious, and trustworthy. Give them your business and they will always find time when you need them. Accompany them when they do the inspection. Learn what they look for and look at. You need to be good at spotting problem areas if you are asked questions. This is a great learning opportunity. Keep quiet and learn.

I PROMISED NO ONE WOULD MISS ME

You know something? This business is infectious and it breeds greed. It's a lot like childbirth; it hurts a lot and takes nearly a year to complete, but as soon as you hold that baby in your arms, you forget the pain and weeks of uneasiness.

Selling my initial one or two homes was tough. I thought I'd never get through it or be able to actually see any money from it. But I did. I actually earned money – a lot of it – and I liked it!!

At the time I thought no amount of money would satisfy my feeling of being abused. Long hours. Crabby sellers. Selfish buyers. Demands on my time. Yet, seeing that commission check made the ill feelings disappear. Success in this business does produce greed, but it's a good greed. It's a greed that speaks to you. It says things like, "Would you rather be selling shoes for the next 6 months to earn the same amount?" Or perhaps you think "They really weren't all that bad even though I did buy them lunch three times and the kids barfed in the car." We tend to forget the missed meals and bedtime stories told by someone other than you.

Initially I promised my husband he'd never miss me. I would do it all: clothes, meals, medical appointments – nothing would be different. I'd handle everything. Who was I kidding? Myself. This is a job. An everyday job and I don't mean an everyday Monday thru Friday, 9-5 kind of job. This is a 9-9 Sunday thru Sunday type of job. The people we work with have jobs. Regular jobs. Jobs that pay regular wages but because of these jobs, they can only look at homes when they are not at work. That means nights – evenings – after dark. I was supposed to play the role of wife, mother and chauffeur after dark. If not me – who would do this? Answer? Their dad, my husband.

I look at it this way, I kept the home fires burning for 13 years before I got my real estate license. I did not work outside the home with the exception of a short lived part time job 2 nights a week so I could earn pocket change. (In reality all I wanted was adult conversation that did not revolve around recipes and diapers.) My husband "kept" me. If I was going to change the dynamics of our home it had better be for the good. I needed incentive!! The answer was easy - I involved all of them in my career and had them all rooting for my success. Each time I sold a house we went out to dinner. After 3 sales, we did something as a family that was special – a weekend at Niagara Falls, tickets to Madison Square Garden and a Broadway play. No longer did anyone resent me going out – they encouraged it.

Weekend open houses were not a pain. I left at noon and came home at 4:00. Dinner was ready and the kids were excited about the people I'd met. My husband developed a new appreciation for the son and daughter he worked so many long hours to support. The kids knew their dad and formed a special relationship they still enjoy. We are a very close family but it took determination, planning and cooperation.

Selling real estate is a business where I may or may not be home at 7:00, but I am home when the kids come home from school and I go to soccer practice, cub scouts and t-ball. I take them to the doctors and we meet for special lunches when there is no school. You see – I control my schedule. An afternoon with my kids is on the schedule as an appointment. My husband wants me to accompany him to a business dinner – he's an appointment. I schedule my life. I manage my business; my business does not manage me. I no longer allow the Buyers or Sellers to schedule my days. I take control. Greed is one thing – family is yet another. Everyone has clean clothes and healthy food. They also have a mom they are very proud of. Now that they are older and have families of their own, we still do family things. Every year my hard work takes us on at least one vacation. We have managed to take vacations with our daughter, her husband and kids, our son, his wife and child. We have relaxed onboard cruise ships and a one-time trip to Las Vegas where we all renewed our wedding vows with Elvis. I've been able to help our children buy homes. In part I hope my tales of negotiations have helped them along the way. After all, they had to learn something listening to my conversations during a number of family dinners.

I remember once my son asked me what I was trying to accomplish during a very long conversation with a Seller who was not being at all flexible. I told him I wanted the Seller to accept my offer but they wanted an additional $5,000. My son looked at me and said, "Mom, 7% of $5,000 is 350 bucks. That's a really good dinner. Try harder!"

CLEAN CLOTHES AT HOME

I've managed to do such a great job of not being missed that my wonderful husband finally told me that doing laundry is easy. What's the big deal? The machine does all the work. As a matter of fact, I'll do it from now on. Wait – what did he just say? He'll do the laundry because it is easy? Who am I to argue. Sorting the colors is a breeze. Selecting the appropriate water temperature – simple. Adding bleach, soap and softener –no problem.

This 'assistance' was great until one of the kids didn't empty their pocket and we had bubblegum washed and dried everywhere. My knit top now fits a three year old. We purchased new white t-shirts to replace the pink ones that met head on with a red striped baseball sock. Yup - laundry is easy.

My husband, never one to admit defeat or frustration, still likes to do the laundry and after all these many years has mastered the chore. Rarely does he shrink or dye our clothing. He's actually trying to turn it into a science. We now have cold water soap, bleach alternatives and dryer sheets. Who'd have guessed dirty clothing could be so interesting. Now if I could only get him to iron. (Truth is – every one of his shirts goes to the cleaners. Washed, pressed, starched, and hung in plastic. Come to think of it - laundry is easy when you only do underwear.)

NO DINNER – WORKING THROUGH DINNER

Not everything in a Realtors' day can be planned and choreographed to run smoothly. Generally it's meal time when the ---- hits the fan in our house. At least it used to... when the kids were home. Now it's pretty easy. We eat when we eat. We eat when we are both home at the same time. We eat out. A lot.

There should be a schedule, but we've become pretty flexible.

Let's back up. Back to the time when the children were home. Back to when I started in this business and I professed my family would never know I was gone. (As hard as it may be to admit, I'm not convinced they ever missed me.)

One thing I learned was to manage my business as a business after the first 2-3 years. Initially, I jumped whenever a Buyer called to see a house which seemed to be as soon as I began cooking the meal or just as I was putting it on the table. Why didn't they call me when I was washing the dishes?

I made appointments when the Seller had their dishes done. Their uninterrupted schedule became my interrupted schedule. After a while I realized if the Buyers and Sellers could make arrangements that suited their lives; why couldn't I do the same. I began to manage my business as a business.

Now that is exactly what I tell agents in my office. The secret to having a life as a Realtor is to manage your time and clients. Do not let the clients manage you.

This is good sound advice. Realtors burn out and they learn to resent the very people you need to be successful. Eventually your frustration will show and the people you should be attracting to work with you and refer you to friends and relatives, will end up distrusting you and your abilities. Seems like you're never around when they need you. Calls are not being answered or returned in a timely fashion. You're not where you should be when you should be there.

When you manage yourself, you will find it an easy task to manage every aspect of your life. You can control the activities of your Buyers and the expectations of the Sellers. If you are responding to their every demand whenever they call – they are controlling you. And when they control you they are controlling your family.

It's important to set up parameters. Tell them when you'll be in touch and stick to that time frame. Let them know when you will be available each and every day. They can always leave a message or email you. Facebook, text or tweet. Tell them how to be in touch. Your clients will be satisfied that they are being heard and you will be in control of your days.

The concept is so simple yet it is rarely implemented.

FINDING SOMEONE LIKE YOU

If you ever plan to get away from your office and take time for yourself and your family – find another agent in your branch office that will treat your business as if it were their business.

I've worked alone, as a partner, as a team member and as a team leader. Every position is interesting and time consuming. If you're a person who likes to be in control – always – you may not work well as a team member. Team leader may be your calling. Every role has its own magnetism.

I needed to find somebody who would take over for me when I took those hard earned family vacations. There were a couple of agents in my office who seemed to handle their client's similarly to the way I worked. They returned phone calls, did open houses and wrote contracts. I realized I could feel comfortable handing over my clients names and needs to one of them. Approach the individual you prefer, but plan ahead. Your proposition should be well defined.

- What are you asking them to do?

- How will they be compensated?

- What happens if your client likes them better?

Having someone cover for you can work as long as each of you understand the demands and responsibilities.

I like having a partner. Partners have a vested interest in your success and failure. Partners want to help the client. They will go the extra mile and never ask why. Your business is treated the same as their business because it is THEIR business (as well as yours.) You can design a partnership to fit your individual roles – keeping in mind everyone must be happy and feel equal.

Being part of a team is just that...equality. Although it is important that one member assume a leadership role. Call him/her the Team Captain. Maybe this role is filled by a more experienced agent who wants to slowly retire but has such a successful Business Base they have leads and referrals aplenty to keep one or two agents in client referrals. The Team Captain/Leader still receives compensation for each lead passed along, but does little, if any, actual sales work.

Another team concept to consider would be one individual handling listings (Sellers) one handling sales (Buyers) and yet another responsible for all of the advertising. As you reflect upon your business record, you will see where your strengths and interests lie. Then you'll know where you should focus your activities to be more satisfied and successful.

You must always remember every Team has an MVP, but without the support and follow-thru of every team member the MVP would look like a three-legged horse in the Kentucky Derby race.

BUILDERS

For short, let's just call them egomaniacs. This group of creative individuals somehow manages to create beautiful, comfortable, living spaces from series of boxes with windows and stairs.

In my area we have an assortment of Builders fitting every need of the Buyer. We have the national builders – doing a beautiful job creating large spaces with all the basics. If you want any of the extras, it costs an additional price. Then there's the Mom & Pop builders who basically make a living remodeling, but will build the entire home if you have the time. This handcrafted experience could take more than a year to complete.

The custom builder has it under control. They usually own the lot, draw the plans, or offer one of several homes designed to fit on the lots in the subdivision. They will take care of every part of the construction – site work, landscaping, flooring, hard surfaces and paint colors. They have a crew where each member has a job.

BEWARE

Don't talk to the workers!!! Usually they are under direct orders from the Builder to work — not talk. In reality, the boss would prefer you not know that the 'subs' (subcontractors — the hired hands of the contractor or builder) were told to use a warped 2X4 or that they had to patch a cracked PVC pipe rather than stop work and order a new one.

If you choose to visit your work site (your future home), be prepared to look past the half-filled paper coffee cups, hamburger wrappers, hundreds of wasted nails and notes scrawled on the walls. Don't be intimidated. By all means you should visit.

These workers are using your money to construct this home. I once heard that a building contractor over ordered wood, shingles, nails, doors — just about everything for each home in the subdivision where he was building. After six or seven months, this family was able to build their own home... cheaply. He was using all of the extras from other jobs!!

Building a home from the ground up is not for the faint of heart. You need to trust your builder and you need to be able to see your floor plans as a finished product. The builder will give advice on doorways and cabinet placement. Remember you need room to open a dishwasher front and a refrigerator door. Place them accordingly. Would you want to look at the toilet every time you sit in the living room? Of course not, but I've been in homes where the buyer never thought about it. I think the best new home story I ever heard was about the builder who went out of town to a wedding. He was gone for only 4 days. Thursday thru Sunday. On that Thursday afternoon, the Buyer decided he would like to move the sliding glass doors leading from the dining room to the deck. The Buyer had seen notes written on the walls before and thought nothing of adding his own request. Unbeknownst to the Builder (away at the wedding), one of his carpenter subs followed the written directions that clearly stated the slider should be moved from the center of the 22 foot room to 14" from the right wall. No problem.

The following Saturday the deck people arrived and proceeded to build the deck according to the original plan. Problem?

On Monday there was a completed deck on the back of the house and a beautifully framed set of sliders leading from the dining room to NOTHING! No one communicated. One hand had no idea what the other had been doing. Who paid for the re-do? Every one. The door installer was fired. The Builder ordered the Buyer to never come back again without an appointment. The only one who did not earn a slap on the wrist was the deck people who did a splendid job - as per instructions.

Building a home is the only way to get a home specific to your needs. Resale homes come with compromises. New construction comes with headaches.

WE ALL WORK TOGETHER

Baloney!! This is the only business I know of where your direct competition is your greatest asset. It would be terrific if we could always sell our own listings, but it is nearly impossible. The moment you enter a listing into the MLS you're inviting every member of the association to bring a buyer. Where can there be a better arrangement? We need these professionals to help us get the job done.

Some agents will make the process a dream. Others, an absolute nightmare. During my career I have always tried to be a cooperative professional who provided as much accurate information as possible. If I said the home had 3 bedrooms and 2 baths, you could bet it had 3 bedrooms and 2 baths and each of those bedrooms had a closet and the bath had a toilet, sink and shower/tub or both. The agents who list homes stating that there are 4-5 bedrooms make me wonder. The 4th bedroom is the office and the 5th the formal dining room. These listing agents should be taken out back and shot. They not only waste our time, but irritate the buyer.

I think the golden rule should prevail in this instance: "Present the listing to others as you would have others present the listing to you." Payback is a bitch but after 28 years, I've found what goes around, comes around. Eventually every one of these cheaters will get their comeuppance. Someone will file an ethics complaint and a fine will be levied. It can be expensive, but it is a lesson to be learned. Our industry must police itself to retain our reputation. We must weed out the bad and train the marginal to care. All of this begins with the Brokers/Managers. Training after you get your license is a must.

WE'RE COUNSELORS & TOUR GUIDES

This just about sums it up. Hop in my car and I'll take you for a ride. When we first meet the Seller we need to counsel them as to the process. They need to know what to expect the moment the FOR SALE sign is planted on the front lawn. We advise them not to talk to the Buyers or the Agents when they come through the home. We advise them to keep the home tidy and clean. We offer advice to make the home seem larger and welcoming and every room appear more spacious. When the Buyer makes the decision to write a purchase contract, we advise and counsel on the plusses and minuses of the offer. We assist in the selection of an attorney. We hold their hands after the home inspection and again at the closing table.

The flip side brings us the opportunity to not only counsel the Buyer with regard to their side of the process, but to advise them regarding market conditions, buyer incentives being offered by lenders, government, et al. They need advice about home inspectors, attorneys, banks and mortgages. They need their hand held throughout the process. Buyers Remorse sets in two days after they find out they will now be paying twice what they paid in monthly rent for their mortgage ....for the next 30 years!

We put on our tour guide hats and show them the local shopping areas, grocery stores, places of worship, parks and museums. If necessary, we can facilitate appointments for the parents to visit the child's school and interview the teachers and principal. We can take them to the bus garage to check out the busses and find out what time the bus will pick up their kid at the end of their driveway, and when they will be safely returned.

A clue to always knowing about bus pick-up and a school assignment, is to talk with the bus garage. The school secretaries will tell you they have no idea which elementary school you will be assigned to until later in the summer. Phooey. The bus drivers know. They know who is going where, when and which way. Skip the administration. Head for the bus garage.

I've incorporated a great coloring book for families who are moving with smaller children. I have a list of utility companies servicing the area. I'll provide new address labels and change of address cards. Whatever comes up – I hope I have it covered. Only once will I get caught off guard not having an answer, a name, or a phone number my client might need. This is what a counselor – a professional – does. Don't make the rest of us look bad. Learn your job.

Learning your job brings us to the next important aspect of this career....

TRAINING

The most important thing I can tell you about training is this: Get it...and get it SOON.

Do yourself and everyone around you a favor – find a company that will train you to do your job and do it correctly. Ask questions. Who conducts the training classes? If the answer is, "You'll be in class with our company trainer", look elsewhere. The answer should be, "We use a group of successful agents and managers who are in the field every day." These are the hard working people you want to learn from. You want their insights and theories. You need to hear the war stories and how each was resolved. I live to hear what went wrong and how it was handled.

Here's a good story you will never hear from a company paid trainer:

I was out showing a home to a lovely young couple. When we approached the home, there was a sign on the door, just above the lockbox. The sign simply stated PLEASE DO NOT LET THE CAT GO OUTSIDE. It was simple request we all thought we could accomplish. We were careful. The old gray cat met us at the door and tried to scamper quickly outside. Not on our watch. Get back in there. We were so careful, each of swore the cat ran in a different direction. We latched the storm door and closed the main entry. When we were ready to leave we glanced around to make certain the cat was nowhere nearby. Success. He was hiding. Great. Get out fast. Upon opening the door – that damn cat was outside on the porch looking in at us. As soon as we stepped on the porch, the shifty critter ran under the bushes. Now, because I am a careful conscientious professional, I knew the cat had to get back in that house. I made the buyers help me catch that cat. Success. As soon as I had it within my grasp I tossed him back inside and slammed the door! Finally. Good riddance.

Around 7:00 that evening I received a call from a woman. "Is this Donna Rausch of xyz realty?" "Yes it is. How can I help you?" "This is Mrs.___ from Elm Street. Were you at my home today showing the house?" Immediately, my first thought was – jeepers, this lady wants to sell her house so badly, she's calling the agents who show her house for feedback. Yuck. {It's not easy to get these calls off the line. If you say something positive, you give them false hope. If you tell them the unbridled truth, they start getting defensive and the conversation never ends well.} "Yes I was there this afternoon." "Did you see my cat?" she asked. "Oh golly. Yes we did and I need to apologize. I have no idea how it escaped, but we found it in the bushes and put it back inside. I hope that's okay." "No it is not okay. My cat is cowering beneath the bed and some filthy muddy cat is making a home on my new sofa!!!"

Have you figured it out yet? It was not the original cat on the porch looking in – it belonged to the neighbor!!!

Sadly, once in a while we do our jobs too well.

MEANS of COMMUNICATING

The key word here is communication. We take classes to understand other people's body language.

- ✓ Mirror your client to gain rapport.
- ✓ Listen carefully.
- ✓ Repeat what you hear for accuracy.
- ✓ Is this personality dominant, analytical, or expressive?
- ✓ Are they listening to you and your message or are they telling you what they want to hear?
- ✓ Are you just trying to get a word into the conversation so you can tell them what you think?

It doesn't matter. What matters is when you meet the client and tell them you will be in touch – do you mean it? You had better.

Years ago we did not have cell phones in our pockets. We needed to make calls from our desks and if we were on the road, we needed money for the pay phone at the corner.

Wow. How times have changed. The 'kids' today have never known a world without a cell phone, without e-mail, without texting, pod casts, webinars, and virtual tours. We have Facebook. We can tweet and we can poke. Messages are on our wall and in our inbox. Life is so...instant. Technology is a wonderful thing. Embrace it. I only stress, if you tell someone that you will get back to them, do it – call them, text them or poke them. You are only as good as your word.

I like cell phones and voice mail. I can leave a message for a client at work. I can get a client who's on the road between point A and B and I can receive and return calls while on vacation.

Email creates a written record of correspondence and conversations. It is wonderfully easy. I can send my client attachments with all the pages of a contract to review without ever having to leave my home or office.

Texting is another improvement to make our lives easier. You do not have to be a great typist or an accomplished speller. I w/c u 2nite @7. C/b w/?'s. TTYL.

(I will call you tonight at 7. Call back with questions. Talk to you later.)

Hieroglyphics? Don't think so. It's text talk. Short and sweet. I can do it in my sleep, while I'm driving (illegal in my state by the way), at the movies or in a meeting. Never out of touch.

How did we get here? Is this even where we want to be? Hell, YES. Only one cautionary word of warning - - - never, and I mean never, write a text or email that says anything you would not say to another person face to face. This is a written log of your words. It is a piece of history when you press send and it cannot be recalled. When speaking to someone, your intonation can change the meaning of your phrasing; a thought being read is open to varied interpretations.

Select a telephone that will do it all. Purchase a plan that will make it affordable. Some dollars you should watch, others? Not so much. Spend the money for a good phone/plan that enables you to be professional and responsible.

HOME NUMBERS and CALLER I.D.

Rarely do I make business calls from my home telephone simply because I do not want the clients to be able to reach me at my residence. I am available 24/7 on my cell phone and everyone I touch has that number. It is the only number on my business card aside from the general office number. There comes a point where you just need a place where you can take off your shoes, put on your pj's, and relax. When I finally do head for home, I call forward my cell to my home number. I will still accept calls at home, but in my clients eyes, I am still out working. If I have to call someone, I only use my cell phone at the house. (Trust me, this is a lesson learned the hard way. If the buyers/sellers think they have another number for you – they will use it.)

Some of my colleagues leave a message on their phones detailing the hours they will be available to return calls.

If you are calling after a certain time in the evening, be prepared to not get a call back until the next day. That's fine. Spell out the way you work and the expectations of your clients will be met. If they are comfortable working under your parameters, there should be no problem. Anyone who is unfamiliar with your rules of running your business may become frustrated – but it's your business. Manage it like a business.

I am certain you're thinking about having your phone numbers restricted. Go ahead. You'll be harder to call back. If I miss your call I will get back to you by using the number that shows up on my phone. If it is restricted? Hmmm. How long may it be before I have the time to track you down?

You left me a message, but half way through your call my call-waiting clicked in and I missed two of your call back numbers. When I listened to your message I was in the car and I goofed when I wrote the number down but erased the message. Can't call you back now, can I? Caller ID allows me to scan my calls and keep your contact information. Make it easy for everyone.

SELLER/BUYER CANNOT BE REAL

Too good to be true? Possibly. There are several scenarios where I question the validity of a client. New York State occasionally sends out TESTERS to check up on the business habits of Realtors. NYS wants to be certain we do not violate rules and the Code of Ethics.

- Did the Realtor follow the Fair Housing guidelines?

- Is the property that was advertised the same property shown at the appointment?

- Did the agent try to show a different area once they had met the caller?

- Was the apartment available when you thought I was not a minority?

Once I had a Buyer call me about a listing. They made an appointment. When they climbed out of the car, they immediately let me know "this was just what they were looking for." They wanted to buy it then and there.

Really?? Honestly?? You don't want to see anything else?? "Nope. This is it."

I was surprised at best. Thought they probably had no money or lousy credit. This just did not happen to me. I had to work hard for my money. It was never this easy. The surprise was on me. They did have cash and they had decent credit. We went all the way to the closing table before they let on they were representatives of a not-for-profit group looking into claims that my company did not treat every buyer fairly. Not against me— against the large firm that I represented. They did this to four agents in the firm. At the closing table, they admitted who they were, forfeited the earnest money deposit, and walked away. No harm done.

Bull____. From that point on, we were all leery of anyone who looked like, smelled like or acted like those imposters. A monumental waste of time to find out we did not discriminate. We were polite and knowledgeable. What they never considered was the cost to the Sellers who thought they had a sale and made plans to move. One even had a contract to purchase another home and a moving van scheduled.

I once met a couple who were living in their camper truck while they attended the local university. They wanted to buy a home because she was expecting and the camper was just too small. Sure. I showed them a few homes and they found one they liked. Another waste of my time but I had been scared by the TESTER so I took everyone out to have a look at homes.

I asked this couple how they planned to pay for the home without jobs. They pulled out an envelope (four envelopes to be more exact) and said they would pay cash. They did. I wrote an offer, got them an attorney, they put $90,000 into the attorneys escrow account and closed 30 days later.

Surprise!! Sometimes it does work out.

TYPES OF BUYERS/SELLERS

Yes, they come in types. Fat, small, rich, poor, fanatically clean and super dirty.

I've been able to identify seven (7) varieties, but I think are many more:

1. **Control Freaks.** This Buyer will tell you what they want to see and how they want to plan the tour. The Seller will tell you how and when to do the open house. Nothing will ever happen on your schedule – only theirs.

2. **Freaky Weirdos.** Every time you meet them it's like you are a stranger. They have a different 'friend' along and pretend to know very little about everything. You wind up constantly wondering if they are smoking something and they have decided not to share.

3. **Nutso-know-it-alls.** I love this breed. No matter what you say they will make it their own. When they hear your answer about schools – they already knew that. They will ask about taxes, only to correct you. They want information but only if they can tell you they already knew that and you have told them nothing new. They are pains. Royal and otherwise.

4. **The Parrots.** This is the one who listens to your answer repeats it verbatim to have validation that they understood you. You can tell them anything and they will say it back to you word for word.

5. **The 'I'm in charge' spouse.** This character only cares about how the move with affect him/her. The job is bringing them here (or forcing them to leave); one of them is delighted and the other is miserable. Too bad. This is for the better. Suffer through it. There is usually zero patience on their part and even less effort to understand.

6. **Delightful and fun.** You want to go out of your way for this group. They love you and you love them. It really doesn't matter if they need to buy or to sell – they are just great to be around. They know this is a move to better the family and are embracing it.

7. **Thankful and gracious.** They buy. They sell. They never thought it would happen especially at that price. You're a miracle worker and a saint. You can be their new best friend. CULTIVATE THESE PEOPLE. They will send referrals to you forever. They can become one of your best resources for future business. If they are as happy as they say they are, they will tell everyone in the company about you. Even the relocation director will know your name.

I have to admit there are probably another two hundred categories for buyers and sellers, but I feel these categories encompass the qualities that seem to dominate the landscape today.

FINALLY... A SELLER

There's an old saying in Real Estate – Realtors never die, they just become list-less.

How true. Listings will be the backbone of your business. This is where you will meet most of the buyers you represent.

You need listings to hold open houses. You need sign calls and you need people to respond to the ads you place.

Working with a Seller is somewhat easier than driving Buyers all over. You meet them, gather information, sign a contract to market their house, put it in the multiple listing and enlist your peers to bring a buyer.

It's as easy as P,P,P:

Plant a sign

Place an ad

Pray.

For the praying aspect – enlist the assistance of St. Joseph. You can buy a statue of St. Joseph in just about any religious store. He comes boxed and the directions for successfully planting him are included. Follow the directions (face up, heading north, front lawn, etc.). There is a prayer included too. Recite it for twelve days and presto! You should have a contract. If only this were true. I have had a statue planted in the lawn of an old listing for over 4 years. Damn thing has yet to sell. Sometimes I think my St. Joseph statue had an expiration date and we have passed it.

Sure there are details you must know in order to fully represent the Seller. You have to do your homework. Know the neighborhood. Be familiar with the schools, churches, shopping. Ask the Seller to tell you the quickest route to the interstate. Where are the usual traffic jams? Be the resource.

Rally your fellow Realtors by having an AGENT ONLY open house. Have food or a drawing. Make it an event. You need your colleagues to help you sell every home you list.

If you are in a Sellers' market, the job may seem easier when you receive a quick full price offer. Conversely, if the Buyers control your market and Sellers have to offer incentives to attracts lookers – get ready to pull out every trick in your bag to get people through the front door. Perhaps you'll offer a higher fee, a selling bonus, offer to pay closing costs. Is it legal in your state to pay the first years taxes for the Buyer?

Is the home properly staged? Do you have an attractive, yet sturdy, For Sale sign? It may be there for a long time. Use the info box. If the home is hard to find – you'll need great directions and corner signs to bring in traffic.

Place the home, with address, on several internet web sites. In other words, advertise the snot out of it!!! Get the home sold.

The only reason you might ever consider taking a listing that is overpriced is if it is on a busy street that will do justice to thousands of people seeing your name every day. We need people to know us and know what we do. Having a sign with your name and phone number attached, is inexpensive advertising. A rider with your photograph is even better.

The Sellers need you to represent their interests. When an offer does come in on the home, you should always deliver the specifics positively. Becoming part of the negatives will get you nowhere. Every line on that contract to purchase should be explained by an excited confident agent who will pass that same feeling of confidence to the Seller. You have been hired to get this home sold and to successfully manage the entire process. Do your job. Come to the negotiating table with confidence and calm.

90

REPRESENTING THAT SELLER

Understand their motivation – why are they uprooting the family dynamic?

Understand their time frame – when do they have to be at the new destination?

Understand their financial position –will they walk away with cash in their hands, need to write a check at the closing to pay off the mortgage, or are they so far underwater that a short sale is the only alternative?

Take great photographs – not good pictures – great pictures. Buyers begin their search on line and visit many sites to find homes that appeal to them. They could discount a wonderful listing just because they did not like the kitchen countertops. Even tho' the countertops look dynamic in the home, the pictures do not do them justice. If you cannot afford a great camera, enlist the help of someone who can help you. Make every picture count. We do not need to see the bathroom with the toilet seat up/down. The beds must be made and the floors clean.

Sellers are incapable of seeing their own dirt and mess. They certainly think the stack of magazines (several months old) beside the lazy-boy lounger that they use to hold the coffee mug every evening is practical. To a Buyer it is the beginning of a Hoarders special!!

Help the Seller stage the home. As a professional we see pitfalls every time we walk into a home. Just because the new baby only sleeps when the television is on is no reason to have a crib in the living room. These Sellers will have to live with discomfort in order to get that sale. When my home was on the market, my kids ate outside on the porch so I could keep the kitchen spotless.

Thankfully it did not rain at all during the 5 days it took to sell.

FINALLY... A BUYER

Can you taste it? Smell it? Have you already made plans how you will spend it or has it already been spent three times over? You have a Buyer and if you play your cards right (ready at their beck and call, full tank of gas, all the answers, and money for coffee and lunch) you will sell them a home and you will get your commission check.

Buyers differ slightly from Sellers. Sellers need to move a commodity. Buyers do not have to buy anything. They can be selective. They can wait until the perfect place pops up. Alternatively, they will simply renew their lease or move back to Mom and Dad's basement.

Where they go is up to YOU. Listen to their wants and needs. Take good notes. Do not talk....listen. And, listen between the lines. They may think they know what they want, until they see something entirely different and fall in love. Happens all the time. Hence the adage: Buyers are Liars.

Set your Buyer up on an automatic notification schedule where every home that is new to the market (or new to them due to a price reduction) is sent directly to their email account. Then rather than walking through 47 homes over a 90 degree weekend, they can drive around and report back to you which ones make the cut. Let them select the BEST 10 and then make appointments to tour those.

**Remember, a note of caution --- have them on a Buyer contract and warn them of what can happen if they enter an open house without their representative.

Years ago, we always represented the Seller and allowed the Buyers to think we were looking out for their best interests. Not always the case and certainly not the legal thing to do. Now in our wisdom, and thanks to the Department of State, Buyers finally have the right to hire an advocate to truly look out for their best interest. Introduce the Buyer to the benefits of a Buyer Agency contract and why they should enter into this contract with you.

REPRESENTING THAT BUYER

At long last, you have entered into a Buyer Agency contract with a lovely couple. You have had an initial meeting with them to discuss the way you conduct your business and they have agreed your structure (or lack thereof) meshes well with their plans and motivation.

Having a signed contract is just the same as having a listing contract to exclusively represent the Seller in the transaction except the table is turned and you are helping a Buyer find a home. You have to be loyal, honest, fair and professional. You are the person with all the answers and if you do not know the answer – find out. You will need to anticipate their concerns before they mention them and have compassion for what they are experiencing.

Walk them through the process:

- When will they be available to look at homes?

- How will you show them the property?

- How many will you look at each time you go out?

- Where will you meet them each time you go out?

- Have you taken them to the bank to be pre-approved?

- Have you counseled them not to enter into any large purchases until after they close?

- Did you talk about 'buyers' remorse'?

- What should they do if they go to an open house?

- Do they have an attorney in mind?
- Of course, they will want a home inspection – do they have anyone in mind?
- Will any one else be coming along?

IT'S YOUR INCOME...SPEND IT

So what are you planning to do with your newly found wealth? Vacation? New clothes? Home addition? Expensive car – no you already have one. How about a vacation property?

Where on your list of planned expenditures did you list "pay your taxes"? Do not forget Uncle Sam. The IRS will be certain to want their fair share.

Because you are considered an independent contractor (by federal definition), your Broker does not take any deductions from your commission checks. It is your sole responsibility to pay state and federal taxes and to contribute to Social Security.

In order to minimize your tax liability you will need to maximize your deductions. That means keeping good records. Retain every receipt when paying for clients meals/snacks; keep receipts when you buy those office supplies and thank you gifts.

The best advice I ever got was to find a good accountant. That's their job. We don't like homeowners who do it themselves (FSBO)because we know more and they should use our expertise. They need us. We need accountants to save us from ourselves and our missed deductions.

Remember in the beginning of this book I mentioned that my family would never miss me. Well, they didn't. But they did miss the good times when the market "turned". We all have lean years and we manage to blame it on everyone and everything except ourselves. Interest rates jumped. The economy stinks. The gas crisis forced prices on everything chemical based to skyrocket.

This is yet another reason to watch your income and expenditures. Budget. Even in slow times, we need to spend money. We still need to advertise properties and ourselves. You can never let the public see you sweat, just be smart about every dollar you invest and invest you should.

Consider buying rental properties. Consider putting money aside for retirement. It doesn't matter if you stay loyal to the same agency for 40 years – there may be a gold watch when you retire, but there typically is no pension plan.

I was lucky. My spouse carried our health insurance. If you do not have that luxury...it's one more thing you will need to consider. Don't forget Disability insurance.

Yes, it is your money and you can finally afford to buy the "stuff" you have only dreamed of, but it may not be all about YOU.

When my kids were applying to colleges, we realized I earned too much money for any kind of financial help. My income placed us in the "you do not get any assistance with college tuition" club. I did not ask to join that club – I earned entry. We paid full shot to the out of state universities for each child. Four years each. Over $20,000 each year. Times two. I wrote tuition checks totaling well over $250,000 including books, housing and meal plans.

Yup, it's my money, and I knew how to spend it! In fact, I still do.

IT'S YOUR LIFE - LIVE IT

You betcha. It's my life and it's been a good one. Once I figured out the basics – it was my life and my career. I had a managing Broker who did his best to form my career and I have a husband, kids and grandchildren who have molded my life. It's worked.

When I was selling, I was successful. When I owned my own company, I was successful. When I was managing, I was successful.

Everything fell in to place because I always worked smart not hard. That's the key. WORK SMART. Don't be the agent who has been in the business for ten years with only one year's experience. Learn and implement. Listen and be advised. Be open and grow.

For the ladies reading this, I give you this comparison:

Selling a home (representing either the Buyer or Seller – or both) is like having a child.

Getting the contracts signed - hearing the Doctor congratulate you on being pregnant. You know there will be frustrations and hardships along the way but it will be worth it in the end.

Angry Buyers/Sellers - merely a bout of morning sickness. It soon will pass.

Open houses/Area tours - swollen ankles and a basketball under your shirt. Part of the experience. Think of the end result.

Negotiations - the beginning of labor. You're close now. Keep pushing.

Closing - bundle of joy. You have just changed people's lives and you received payment for doing it.

The end result far outweighs the uncomfortable feelings and the worries. If it didn't, Adam and Eve would have been the original and only homeowners and no one ever would have more than one offspring.

Enjoy your life. It can be terrific but it will be work.

Remember, Real Estate is simple.

It's just not easy !!

ABOUT THE AUTHOR

Donna Rausch has been a Realtor since 1985. Over the course of her career she has worked as a sales agent, associate broker, broker/manager and a broker/owner.

Accomplished in her sales career, Donna ranked among the top 10 Realtors in her Association for over 2/3 of her career. Now she works as a branch manager for two independent offices and as one of several trainers for the company.

Donna also served as a Director and Board President of her local Association. Over the years, she has served on the Grievance and Professional Standards panels, Legislative and Finance committees, and Multiple Listing Service Board of Directors. In 2012 her Association named her Broker Manager of the Year. In 2013, Donna was elected to serve as the Central New York Regional VP for the New York State Association of Realtors.

In her free time she and her husband travel whenever they can having been to over 25 countries around the world. Her family, including her four grandchildren, make the hard work even more worthwhile.

www.ingramcontent.com/pod-product-compliance
Lightning Source LLC
Chambersburg PA
CBHW071227170526
45165CB00003B/1018